香港國際詩歌之夜 2013
INTERNATIONAL POETRY NIGHTS IN HONG KONG

編輯 Editors

北島 Bei Dao

陳嘉恩 Shelby K. Y. Chan

方梓勳 Gilbert C. F. Fong

柯夏智 Lucas Klein

馬德松 Christopher Mattison

李晟馥
Lee Seong-bok

目錄 Contents

1 1959년

그해 겨울이 지나고 여름이 시작되어도
봄은 오지 않았다 복숭아나무는
채 꽃 피기 전에 아주 작은 열매를 맺고
不姙의 살구나무는 시들어 갔다
소년들의 性器에는 까닭없이 고름이 흐르고
의사들은 아프리카까지 移民을 떠났다 우리는
유학 가는 친구들에게 술 한잔 얻어 먹거나
이차 대전 때 南洋으로 징용 간 삼촌에게서
뜻밖의 편지를 받기도 했다 그러나 어떤
놀라움도 우리를 無氣力과 不感症으로부터
불러내지 못했고 다만, 그 전해에 비해
약간 더 화려하게 절망적인 우리의 습관을
修飾했을 뿐 아무 것도 追憶되지 않았다
어머니는 살아 있고 여동생은 발랄하지만
그들의 기쁨은 소리 없이 내 구둣발에 짓이겨
지거나 이미 파리채 밑에 으깨어져 있었고
春畫를 볼 때마다 부패한 채 떠올라 왔다
그해 겨울이 지나고 여름이 시작되어도
우리는 봄이 아닌 倫理와 사이비 學說과
싸우고 있었다 오지 않는 봄이어야 했기에
우리는 보이지 않는 監獄으로 자진해 갔다

1959年

那年冬天過後就是夏天
春天沒有來　桃樹
還沒開花就結出小小的果實
不孕的杏樹枯萎了
少年們的性器無緣無故地流出膿水
醫生們移民非洲　出國
留學的朋友請我們喝酒
意外地收到二戰期間
被征到南洋的叔叔的信　任何
驚訝都不能將我們從無力和麻木中
喚醒　我們只是
修飾著比前年更華麗的絕望習慣
沒有任何回憶
媽媽還活著　妹妹活力四射
她們的喜悅卻被我的皮鞋無聲地踐踏
或者早已撚碎在蒼蠅拍下
每次看春畫的時候才會腐朽地湧起
那年冬天過後就是夏天
我們和沒有春天的邏輯鬥爭　和似是而非
的學說鬥爭　春天還是沒有來
我們自覺地走向看不見的監獄

（薛舟譯）

1959

that year, though winter ended and summer began
spring did not come   the peach tree
bore tiny fruits before flowering
and the barren apricot withered
for unknown reasons pus oozed from the penises of
young boys
and doctors emigrated as far as Africa   we were
treated to drinks by
friends leaving to study abroad
and out of the blue a letter arrived from an uncle
drafted
and sent to the South Pacific during World War Two
but there were
no surprises to roust us from our indifference and
apathy
and other than glamorizing,
even more than last year, our habitual depression,
we did nothing worth remembering
mom was still alive and my younger sister full of life,
yet without a peep from them their happiness was
squashed,

beneath my shoes, by flyswatters—a memory that
  surfaced,
rotten, whenever I saw a salacious picture
though winter ended and summer began
it wasn't the spring we wrestled with, but ethics
and false theories   it was a spring that did not
  come,
and so we voluntarily went off to an invisible jail

(Translated by Hye-jin Juhn Sidney & George Sidney)

2 出埃及

1

오늘 다 외로와하면
내일 씹을 괴로움이 안 남고
내일 마실 그리움이 안 남는다
오늘은 집에 돌아가자 세편의 映畫를 보고
두 명의 주인공이 살해되는 꼴을 보았으니
운좋게 살아남은 그 녀석을 너라 생각하고
집에 돌아가자, 살아 있으니
수줍어 말고 되돌아 취하지 말고 돌아가자
돌아가 싱싱한 떡잎으로 자라나서
훨훨 날아올라 충격도, 마약도 없이
꿈 속에서 한 편 映畫가 되어 펼쳐지자

2

내가 떠나기 전에 길은 제 길을 밟고
사라져 버리고, 길은 마른 오징어처럼
펴져 있고 돌이켜 술을 마시면
먼저 취해 길바닥에 드러눕는 愛人

나는 퀭한 地下道에서 뜬눈을 새우다가
헛소리하며 찾아오는 東方博士들을
죽일까봐 겁이 난다

이제 집이 없는 사람은 天國에 셋방을 얻어야
하고
사랑받지 못하는 사람은 아직 欲情에 떠는 늙
은 子宮으로 돌아가야 하고
忿怒에 떠는 손에 닿으면 문둥이와 앉은뱅이까
지 낫는단다, 主여

出埃及

一

今天的孤獨享盡之後
就不會留下明天咀嚼的痛苦
也不會留下明天飲嘗的思念
今天回家吧　看了三部電影
看到兩名主人公被害的慘狀
把那個倖存的傢伙想成是你
回家吧　既然你還活著
就不要害羞　不要喝醉　回家吧
回家　長成茂盛的子葉
翩翩飛舞　沒有衝擊　沒有毒品
成為一部電影　展現在夢裏

二

我出發之前　路踩著自己的路
消失　路像乾魷魚
延伸　轉彎　每次喝酒
總是醉臥在路邊的愛人

我在空蕩蕩的地下道裏徹夜未眠
我害怕
自己會殺死胡言亂語找來的東方博士

如今沒有家的人只能在天國租房
得不到愛的人只能回到仍在情欲中顫抖的衰老的子
宮
只要碰到因憤怒而顫抖的手　麻風病人和癱子也能
痊癒，主啊

（薛舟譯）

exodus

1

if you consume all your loneliness today
you won't have any pain left to chew on tomorrow
you won't have any longing left to drink tomorrow
as for today, let's go home   you've watched three
films
and seen two main characters murdered
so let me think the lucky one who survived is you
and let's go home   you're alive, so
let's not be self-conscious or go off to get drunk but
let's go home and then fresh as young leaves let's
fly up to the sky   not from drugs, or from the
shocks we've had, but
from our dreams let's spin out a movie

2

even before I start off the road, treading on itself,
vanishes   it lies flat like dried squid
I turn back and drink
my girl friend gets drunk first and sprawls on the
ground

I'm afraid that having stayed awake all night
in the murk of an underpass I'll kill the Three Wise
  Men
when they come talking nonsense

now those who don't have homes should rent rooms in
  heaven
and those who aren't loved should return to old wombs
  still quivering with lust
and even lepers and cripples will be cured if touched by
  a hand that shakes with wrath, my Lord

(Translated by Hye-jin Juhn Sidney & George Sidney)

3 여름산

여름산은 솟아 오른다
熱氣와 金屬의 투명한 옷자락을 끌어 올리며
솟아 오른다 발등에 못 안 박힌 것들은 다 솟
　　아 오른다 저기
비행기가 수술톱처럼 하늘을 끊어낸다 은빛 날개
　　가 곤두선다
그 여자는 佛蘭西에 가겠다고 이번 여름엔 꼭
다녀와야겠다고 그 여자는 잠자는 벌레를 밟았
　　다 모르고
밟았다 부서지면서 물 같은 피가 솟아 올랐다 내
　　가 거듭 밟았다
그 여자는 佛蘭西에 가겠다고

나는 속으로 욕했다
따지고 보면 욕할 이유가 없었다
당신은 남의 가난이 얼마큼 당신과 관계 있다고 생
　　각합니까
그 여자는 내가 가난한 사람이 아니라고 말했다
당신은 백 사람 중에 하나가 병들어 아프면 당신
　　도 아프다고 생각합니까
그 여자는 부질없는 말이라고 대답했다

여름산은 솟아 오른다
여름산은 땀 흘리지 않는다 힘쓰지 않는다
여름산 여름산 여름산 우리는 그늘에서 콜라를 마
셨다
콜라를 마시며 佛蘭西를 생각하고 울었다 우는 시
늉을 했다
우리는, 시멘트 포를 등에 지고 사다리 오르는 여
인들을 생각하며 울었다
우는 흉내를 냈다 우리는, 바빌론에 묶여 있는 이
스라엘 사람들을 생각하며 울었다 우는 척했다

여름산은 솟아 오른다
한숨 쉬지 않고 솟아 오른다 반짝임과 몽롱함을 뿌
리며 솟아 오른다
우리는 손을 잡았다 잡힌 손에서 물 같은 피가 흘
렀다 살려줘요!

여름산은 무겁게 솟아 오른다
솟아 오르지 않는다 솟아 오르는 모습만 보여 준다
여름산 여름산 여름산 먼지, 매연, 악취로 부서지는

여름산 여름산
여름산

夏天的山

夏天的山高聳
掀起熱氣和金屬的透明衣角
高聳　腳背沒釘釘子的東西全部高聳
飛機像手術刀　切開天空　豎起銀翼

她說要去法蘭西　今年夏天
非去不可　她踩到睡著的蟲子卻不知道
蟲子被踩碎　冒出水似的血　我又踩上了
她說要去法蘭西

我在心裏咒罵
仔細想來　我沒理由罵人
你認為別人的貧窮和你有什麼關係
她說我不是窮人
百分之一的人生病　你會感覺痛苦嗎
她說這是無稽之談

夏天的山高聳
夏天的山努力不流汗
夏天的山　夏天的山　夏天的山　我們在陰涼裏喝
　　可樂

喝著可樂　想著法蘭西哭泣　模仿哭泣
我們，想到背著水泥袋爬梯子的女人而哭泣
模仿哭泣　我們想到被綁在巴比倫的以色列人而哭
　　泣　假裝哭泣

夏天的山高聳
一刻不停地高聳　噴灑著璀璨和朦朧　高聳
我們手拉手　手裏流出水樣的鮮血　救命啊！

夏天的山沉重地高聳
不是高聳　只是顯出高聳的模樣
夏天的山　夏天的山　夏天的山　因為灰塵　煤煙
　　和惡臭
而粉碎的夏天的山　夏天的山
夏天的山

（薛舟譯）

the summer mountain

the summer mountain rises
dragging along its transparent vestments of heat and
  metal
it rises   all whose feet are not nailed down rise too
above, like a surgical saw a plane rips the sky   its
  silver wings angled upward

the woman insisted she'd go to France   she'd go this
  summer
for sure   she stepped on a sleeping bug   not
  knowing it was there
she stepped on it   as it cracked, liquid like blood
  shot up   I too
stepped on it   she insisted she would go to France

I felt critical of her
but reflecting on it there was no reason to be critical of
  her
how much does the poverty of others mean to you?
she said I wasn't poor

if only one in a hundred is sick and in pain, can you also feel the pain?
senseless questions, she said

the summer mountain rises
the summer mountain doesn't sweat   it doesn't exert itself
the summer mountain the summer mountain the summer mountain   we drank cola in the shade
as we drank we cried, thinking of France   we pretended to cry
we cried thinking of the working women climbing ladders with sacks of cement on their backs
we pretended to cry   we cried thinking of the Israelites in captivity in Babylon   we pretended to cry

the summer mountain rises
without taking a breath it rises   shattering shadow and light it rises

we held each other's hands blood flowed from our
hands help!

the summer mountain rises ponderously
it doesn't rise it generates the illusion that it is
rising
the summer mountain the summer mountain the
summer mountain obliterated by dust, exhaust
fumes, toxic stench
the summer mountain the summer mountain
the summer mountain

(Translated by Hye-jin Juhn Sidney & George Sidney)

4 그해 가을

그해 가을 나는 아무에게도 便紙 보내지 않았지만
늙어 軍人 간 친구의 便紙 몇 통을 받았다 세
　　상 나무들은
어김없이 동시에 물들었고 풀빛을 지우며 집들
　　은 언덕을
뻗어나가 하늘에 이르렀다 그해 가을 濟州産 5년
　　생 말은
제 주인에게 대드는 자가용 운전사를 물어뜯었
　　고 어느
유명 작가는 南美紀行文을 연재했다
아버지, 아버지가 여기 계실 줄 몰랐어요
그해 가을 소꿉장난은 國産映畫 보다 시들했으
　　며 길게
하품하는 입은 더 깊고 울창했다 깃발을 올리거
　　나 내릴
때마다 말뚝처럼 사람들은 든든하게 박혔지만 햄머
휘두르는 소리, 들리지 않았다 그해 가을 모래
　　내 앞
샛강에 젊은 뱀장어가 떠오를 때 파헤쳐진 샛강
　　도 둥둥
떠올랐고 高架道路 공사장의 한 사내는 새 깃털

과 같은
速度로 떨어져내렸다 그해 가을 개들이 털갈이
할 때
지난 여름 번데기 사 먹고 죽은 아이들의 어머니
는 후미진
골목길을 서성이고 실성한 늙은이와 天賦의 白痴
는
서울역이나 창경원에 버려졌다 그해 가을 한 승려
는
人骨로 만든 피리를 불며 密教僧이 되어 돌아왔
고 내가
만날 시간을 정하려 할 때 그 여자는 침을 뱉
고 돌아섰다
아버지, 새벽에 나가 꿈 속에 돌아오던 아버지,
여기 묻혀 있을 줄이야
그해 가을 나는 세상에서 재미 못 봤다는 투의 말
버릇은
버리기로 결심했지만 이 결심도 농담 이상의 것은
아니었다 떨어진 은행잎이나 나둥그러진 매미를 주
워
성냥갑 속에 모아두고 나도 누이도 房門을 안으로

잠갔다 그해 가을 나는 어떤 가을도 그해의 것이
아님을 알았으며 아무것도 美化시키지 않기 위해서
는
卑下시키지도 않는 法을 배워야 했다
아버지, 아버지! 내가 네 아버지냐
그해 가을 나는 살아온 날들과 살아갈 날들
을 다 살아
버렸지만 壁에 맺힌 물방울 같은 또 한 女子를 만
났다
그 여자가 흩어지기 전까지 세상 모든 눈들이 감기
지
않을 것을 나는 알았고 그래서 그레고르 잠자의 家
族들이
移葬을 끝내고 소풍 갈 준비를 하는 것을 이해했
다
아버지, 아버지...... 씹새끼, 너는 입이 열이라
도 말 못해
그해 가을, 假面 뒤의 얼굴은 假面이었다

那年秋天

那年秋天　我沒有給誰寫過信
卻收到幾封來自老了才去參軍的朋友的信　世上的
　　樹木
不約而同地同時染色　抹掉了綠　房子沿著山坡
伸展　直達天空　那年秋天　產自濟州的五年生馬
　　匹
咬了頂撞主人的車夫　某個
著名作家在連載《南美紀行文》
父親，我不知道父親在這裏
那年秋天　過家家比國產電影還無聊　長長地
打著哈欠的嘴更加深邃和蒼茫　每當升旗降旗
的時候　人們就像牢牢釘緊的木樁　卻聽不見
揮舞錘子的聲音　那年秋天　當小鰻魚浮上
沙河前的沙洲　被挖開的沙洲
也悠悠浮起　在高架路施工現場　一個男人
以羽毛的速度墜落　那年秋天　狗換毛的時候
夏天吃蛹而死的孩子們的媽媽在僻靜的
胡同裏徘徊　精神失常的老人和天生的白癡
被人拋棄在首爾火車站和昌慶苑　那年秋天　一位
　　和尚
吹著用人骨做成的笛子　變成密教僧侶歸來

我要確定見面的時間　那個女人啐了口唾沫　轉過
　　身去
父親，清晨出門又在夢中歸來的父親，
誰能想到他會被埋在這裏
那年秋天　我決心要改掉這個世界真沒勁
的口頭禪　不過這決心也只是
開個玩笑　我撿起凋零的銀杏葉和跌落的蟬
積攢在火柴盒裏　我和姐姐反鎖了房門
那年秋天　我知道哪個秋天也不屬於
那一年　為了不美化任何事物
我必須學會不醜化的方法
父親，父親！我是你的父親嗎
那年秋天　從前的日子和未來的日子
我都已過完　卻遇到了像是牆上凝結的水珠的女人
我知道　那個女人消散之前　世界上所有的眼睛
都不會關閉　我理解格雷戈爾·薩姆沙的家人們
移葬結束　做好了出門郊遊的準備
父親，父親……兔崽子，你跳進黃河也洗不清了
那年秋天　面具背後的臉還是面具

（薛舟譯）

that fall

that fall though I didn't send anybody a letter   I got
several from
friends who'd gone off to do the obligatory military
service they'd been
postponing   all the trees in the world turned yellow
at the same time,
as usual, and houses scaled the hillside right up to the
sky, overwhelming
the color of grass   that fall a five-year-old Cheju
Island pony bit
somebody's private chauffeur arguing with its owner,
and a well-known
writer serialized some travel pieces about his journey to
South America
Dad, I didn't realize you were going to be here
that fall the children playing house were more tedious
even than
Korean films, and the long drawn-out yawns were
heavier   whenever we
raised the flag or lowered it people were driven like
posts into the ground,

but the sound of a hammer wasn't heard   that fall when a dead
young eel floated to the surface of the stream in front of Moraenae,
the stream, which had been dredged, also floated, and a worker fell
at the speed of a feather from the elevated expressway that was being
built   that fall when dogs changed coats, the mother of the children
who'd died the previous summer after eating sautéed silkworm larvae
bought from a sidewalk vendor, hung out on dark street corners
a senile old man was abandoned at the Seoul train station,
as was a congenital idiot at the Changgyeong Palace   that fall a
Buddhist monk returned as a mystic, playing a flute made of human
bone, and when I asked a woman for a date she spit

and turned away
my father, who used to leave home in the early
morning and come back
in my dreams, how would I have known he was buried
here
that fall I decided to break my habit of talking as
though there wasn't
any fun in my life, but even that decision turned out to
be no more
than a joke I picked up fallen ginkgo leaves and
dead cicadas and kept
them in match boxes, and my sister and I locked our
rooms from inside
that fall I realized there was no fall that belonged to
any particular year
and I taught myself not to debase things so as not to
beautify them
Dad, Dad! Am I your dad
that fall I lived all the days I'd lived, and those I was
going to live
but I met another woman, who was like a drop of

water clinging
to a wall, and I realized that not an eye in all the world
would close
until she splattered, so I understood why Gregor
Samsa's family
prepared to go on an outing after burying him
Dad, Dad ... you little fucker, you should be too
ashamed to talk
that fall, the face behind the mask was a mask

(Translated by Hye-jin Juhn Sidney & George Sidney)

5 세월에 대하여

1

石手의 삶은 돌을 깨뜨리고 채소 장수의 삶은
하루 종일 서 있다 몬티를 닮은 내 친구는
同時上映館에서 죽치더니 또 어디로 갔는지
세월은 갔고 세월은 갈 것이고 이천 년 되는 해
아침 나는 孫子를 볼 것이다 그래 가야지
天國으로 통하는 車들은 바삐 지나가고
가로수는 줄을 잘 맞춘다 저기, 웬 아이가
쥐꼬리를 잡고 빙빙 돌리며 씽긋 웃는다
세월이여, 얼어붙은 날들이여
야근하고 돌아와 환한 날들을 잠자던 누이들이여

2

피로의 물줄기를 타넘다 보면 때로 이마에
뱀딸기꽃이 피어 오르고 그건 대부분
幻影이었고 때로는 정말 형님이 아들을 낳기도
했다 아버지가 으흐허 웃었다 발가벗은
나무에서 또 몇 개의 열매가 떨어졌다 때로는
얼음 깔린 하늘 위로 붉은 말이 연탄을
끌고 갔다 그건 대부분 幻影이었고 정말
허리 꺾인 아이들이 철 지난 고추나무처럼

언덕에 박혀 있기도 했다 정말 去勢된
친구들이 유행가를 부르며 사라져 갔지만
세월은 흩날리지 않았다 세월은 신다 버린 구두
속에서 곤한 잠을 자다 들키기도 하고
때로는 총알 맞은 새처럼 거꾸로 떨어졌다
아버지는 으흐허 웃고만 있었다 피로의 물줄기를
타넘다 보면 때로 나는 높은 새집 위에서
잠시 쉬기도 하였고 그건 대부분 幻影이었다

3

세월은 갔고 아무도 그 어둡고 깊은 노린내 나는
구멍으로부터 돌아오지 못했다 몇 번인가 되돌아온
便紙 해답은 언제나 질문의 殘骸였고 친구들은
태엽 풀린 비행기처럼 고꾸라지곤 했다 너무
피곤해 手淫을 할 수 없을 때 어른거리던
하얀 풀뿌리 얼어붙은 웅덩이 세월은 갔고
매일매일 작부들은 노래 불렀다 스물 세 살,
스물 네 살 나이가 담뱃진에 노랗게 물들 때까지
또 나는 열 한 시만 되면 버스를 집어 탔고

세월은 갔다 봉제 공장 누이들이 밥 먹는 30분 동
안
다리미는 세워졌고 어느 예식장에서나 30분마다
신랑 신부는 바뀌어 갔다 세월은 갔다 변색한
백일 사진 華僑들의 공동묘지 싸구려 밥집 빗물
고인 길바닥, 나뭇잎에도 세월은 갔다 한 아이가
세발 자전거를 타고 번잡한 찻길을 가고 있었다
어떤 사람은 불쌍했고 어떤 사람은 불쌍한
사람을 보고 울었다 아무 것도 그 비리고 어지러운
숨막힌 구멍으로부터 돌아오지 못했다

4
나는 세월이란 말만 들으면 가슴이 아프다
나는 곱게곱게 자라왔고 몇 개의 돌부리 같은
事件들을 제외하면 아무 일도 없었다 중학교
고등학교 그 어려운 修業時代, 욕정과 영웅심과
부끄러움도 쉽게 風化했다 잊어버릴 것도 없는데
세월은 안개처럼, 醉氣처럼 올라온다
웬 들 판 이 이 렇 게 넓 어 지 고
얼마나빨간작은꽃들이지평선끝까지아물거리는가

그해
자주 눈이 내리고
빨리 흙탕물로 변해갔다
나는 밤이었다 나는 너와 함께
기차를 타고 민둥산을 지나가고 있
었다 이따금 기차가 멎으면 하얀 物體가
어른거렸고 또 기차는 떠났다 ...... 세월은 갔다

어쩌면 이런 일이 있었는지도 모른다

내가
돌아서
출렁거리는
어둠 속으로 빨려들어갈 때
너는 발을 동동 구르며
부서지기 시작했다
아무 소리도 들리지 않았다

(나는 너를 사랑했다
나는 네가 잠자는 두 평 房이었다
人形 몇 개가 같은 표정으로 앉아 있고

액자 속의 教會에서는 종소리가 들리
는 ...... 나는 너의 房이었다
네가 바라보는 풀밭이었다
풀밭 옆으로 숨죽여 흐르는 냇물이었다
그리고 나는 아무 것도 아니었다
문득 고개를 떨군 네
마음 같은,
한줌
空氣였다)

세월이라는 말이 어딘가에서 나를 발견할 때마다
하늘이 눈더미처럼 내려앉고 전깃줄 같은 것이
부들부들 떨고 있는 것을 본다 남들처럼
나도 두어 번 戀愛에 실패했고 그저 실패했을
뿐, 그때마다 유행가가 얼마만큼 절실한지
알았고 노는 사람이나 놀리는 사람이나 그리
행복하지 않다는 것을 알아야 했다 세월은
언제나 남보다 앞서 갔고 나는 또 몇 번씩
그 비좁고 습기찬 門間을 지나가야 했다

關於歲月

一

石匠的人生就是打碎石頭　菜販子的人生
是站立終日　酷似蒙蒂的朋友
泡在同時上映館　這會兒不知去了哪裏
歲月流逝　歲月還會繼續流逝　已是兩千年
的早晨　我會看到孫子　是的　我要去
通往天國的車忙忙碌碌
行道樹排列整齊　那裏　有個孩子
抓著老鼠尾巴團團轉圈　面帶微笑

歲月啊　冰封的日子
夜班歸來　姐姐們在燦爛的白天酣然入睡

二

跨過疲憊的水柱　有時額頭上
會開出蛇梅花　大部分
是幻影　有時哥哥真的會生孩子
父親哈哈笑　赤裸裸的
樹上又掉落幾顆果實　有時
紅馬拉著煤炭走向冰封的天空
這些大部分是幻影

彎腰的孩子們真的像過季的辣椒秧
插滿山坡　被閹割的朋友們真的
唱著流行歌曲消失　不過
歲月不會飄散　歲月在穿破扔掉的皮鞋裏
熟睡　有時被發現
有時像中彈的小鳥　倒頭跌落
父親只是哈哈笑　跨過疲憊的水柱
有時我在高高的鳥巢裏
休息片刻　這些大部分是幻影

三

歲月流逝　誰也不能從黑暗深邃而腥臭
的洞中返回　幾次被退回的信
總是疑問的殘骸　朋友們
就像發條鬆弛的飛機　倒栽下來
疲憊得無力手淫的時候　冰凍的水坑裏
白色的草根在搖曳　歲月流逝
妓女們每天唱歌　直到二十三歲
二十四歲的年紀被香煙薰黃
每天夜裏十一點　我就乘上公車

歲月流逝　縫紉機廠的姐姐們吃飯的三十分鐘裏
熨斗被豎起　無論是哪個禮堂　每隔三十分鐘
新郎新娘都會被換掉　歲月流逝　褪色的
百日照　華僑公墓　廉價飯館
積了雨水的路面　歲月也在樹葉上流逝　一個孩子
騎著三輪自行車　走過雜亂的車道
有人很可憐　有人為可憐的人
哭泣　一切都不能從那血腥凌亂
令人窒息的洞中返回

四

我聽到歲月這個字眼就會心痛
我從小備受寵愛　除了幾塊
絆腳石　基本上平安無事　中學
困難的學習時代　情欲和英雄心
和羞恥都輕易地風化　沒什麼需要遺忘
歲月像霧，像醉意繚繞
為 什 麼 田 野 變 得 如 此 遼 闊
那麼紅的小花輕輕搖曳直到地平線盡頭

那年
經常下雪
迅速地化作泥湯
我是黑夜　和你一起
乘坐火車 翻過荒山野嶺
偶爾火車停下　白色的物體
閃爍　火車又開了……歲月流逝

也許發生過這樣的事情

我
轉身
被吸入
激蕩的黑暗
你咚咚跺腳
開始粉碎
什麼聲音也聽不見

（我愛你
我是你睡覺的兩坪的房子
幾個玩偶面帶同樣的表情端坐

鏡框裏的教堂　鐘聲響起……
我是你的房子
是你凝望的草地
是草地邊屏息流淌的溪水
然而我什麼都不是
我是
一縷空氣
像你的心
當你忽然低頭的時候）

當歲月這個詞在某個地方發現我
天空如雪堆降落　電線似的東西
看著什麼在瑟瑟發抖　像別人
我也兩三次戀愛失敗　失敗而已
這時　我會知道流行歌曲是多麼真實
我必須懂得　玩弄的人和被玩弄的人
都不幸福　歲月
總是走在別人前面　我還要幾次
通過那個狹窄而潮濕的門檻

（薛舟譯）

about time

1

a mason's life is breaking stone and a grocer's life is
   standing
all day   my friend who looked like Montgomery
   Clift used to
hang around a third-class double-feature movie house
I don't know what's become of him   time has passed
   and will
continue to pass   on the morning of the first day of
   the year
two thousand I'll have a grandson   well, I've got to
   go   the cars
to paradise flash past, the roadside trees stand in
   straight rows
over there a child grins, twirling a mouse by its tail

time, frozen days   sisters who after working all
   night at the factory
slept through sun-bright days

2

as I followed the river of weariness, from time to time
on my
forehead a wild strawberry bloomed most of that
was fantasy
in reality from time to time my elder brother sired a
son
laughter burbled from my father again some fruit
fell
from a naked tree from time to time a red horse
crossed
the iced-over sky pulling a cartload of *yeontan*
briquettes
most of that was fantasy in reality some children,
bent double,
were rooted on a hill like red-pepper plants left
uncollected during
harvest in reality my emasculated friends
disappeared singing
current pop songs but time did not fly away
it was sometimes found deeply asleep inside a worn

abandoned shoe
and from time to time it plummeted upside down
like a shot-gunned bird   laughter burbled from my
father
as I followed the river of weariness from time to time I
rested
upon a bird's nest high up   most of that was fantasy
too

3

time passed and nobody was able to come back from
the deep dark
stinking hole   a letter was returned several times
answers were always
to be found in the debris of questions and friends
would give out
like toy airplanes with spent rubber-bands   when I
was too tired to
masturbate the white roots of grass in a frozen swamp
swam before
my eyes   time passed   the prostitutes sang songs

every day, and by the
time they were twenty-three, twenty-four, cigarettes
had stained them
yellow   and every night by eleven I caught the bus
for home

and time passed   during the half hour the girls at
the sewing
factory ate lunch the clothes irons stood cooling and
every half hour
in every wedding hall there was another bride and
groom
time passed   in an infant's faded hundredth-day
photo   in a public
graveyard for Chinese immigrants   in a cheap
restaurant   on a road
where rainwater puddle   on leaves   time passed
on a street busy with traffic a child pedaled along on a
tricycle
some people were miserable, some who saw them wept
nothing could come back from the asphyxiating

malodorous dizzying hole

4

my heart aches whenever I hear the word time
I was brought up as a treasured child, and nothing significant
happened to me other than my encountering in my path
a few stones that I got easily past—middle school, high school,
the difficult period of learning, and then lust, and a desire to be heroic,
and feelings of shame   though there's nothing I need to forget,
time rises like a fog, like drunkenness
how   is   it   that   the   field   grows   so   wide
andhowisitthattherearesomanyredflowerswaveringonthe horizon

that year
snow fell often and
the road turned quickly muddy
I was night, I was on a train with you
passing a bare mountain   the train
from time to time stopped, something white
flickered, and the train moved on again … time passed

this also might have happened

when I
turned round
and sank into
the rolling darkness
stamping the ground
you began to break apart
not a sound
was heard

(I loved you

I was the two-*pyeong* room you were sleeping in
several dolls with the same face sat next to each other
and a bell tolled in the church inside a framed picture ...
I was your room
I was the grassy field you gazed at
I was the stream that ran quietly alongside the grassy field
and I was nothing
I was
a handful of air,
like your heart
when of a sudden you bow your head)

whenever the word time comes upon me somewhere
I see the sky falling like an avalanche of snow
and something like an electric wire
vibrating   like others
I several times failed at love   each time was only
a failure   I came to understand how touching pop
songs
can be and that neither the toyed with

nor the toyers are happy   time always
ran ahead of me and over and over again I had to
pass through a narrow damp space between doors

(Translated by Hye-jin Juhn Sidney & George Sidney)

6 이제는 다만 때 아닌, 때 늦은 사랑에 대하여

이제는 송곳보다 송곳에 찔린 허벅지에 대하여
말라붙은 눈꺼풀과 문드러진 입술에 대하여
정든 유곽의 맑은 아침과 식은 아랫목에 대하여
이제는, 정든 유곽에서 빠져 나올 수 없는 한 발자
　　국을
위하여 질퍽이는 눈길과 하품하는 굴뚝과 구정물
　　에 흐르는
종소리를 위하여 더럽혀진 처녀들과 비명에 간 사
　　내들의
썩어가는 팔과 꾸들꾸들한 눈동자를 위하여 이제는
누이들과 처제들의 꿈꾸는, 물 같은 목소리에 취하
　　여
버려진 조개 껍질의 보라색 무늬와 길바닥에 쓰러
　　진
까치의 암록색 꼬리에 취하여 노래하리라 정든 유
　　곽
어느 잔칫집 어느 상갓집에도 찾아다니며 피어나고
떨어지는 것들의 낮은 신음 소리에 맞추어 녹은 것
구부러진 것 얼어붙은 것 갈라터진 것 나가떨어
　　진 것들

옆에서 한 번, 한 번만 보고 싶음과 만지고 싶음
과 살 부비고 싶음에
관하여 한 번, 한 번만 부여안고 휘이 돌고 싶음
에 관하여
이제는 다만 때 아닌, 때 늦은 사랑에 관하여

現在只說遲到的愛來得不是時候

現在要說的不是錐子而是被錐子刺中的大腿
是乾涸的眼皮和破爛的嘴唇
是日久生情的妓院晴朗的早晨和冷卻的炕頭
現在為了無法從日久生情的妓院邁出的腳印
為了泥濘的雪路和哈欠連天的煙囪和污水中
流淌的鐘聲　為了被玷污的處女和死於悲鳴的男子
　　漢們
腐爛的手臂和硬邦邦的眼珠　現在
陶醉於姐姐和小姨子們夢中如水的聲音
陶醉於貝殼的紫紋和躺在路上的喜鵲
的暗綠色尾巴　歌唱　在日久生情的妓院
在喜宴人家和喪事人家也綻放和凋落的事物
配合著它們低沉的呻吟而溶化的事物
彎曲的　冰凍的　崩裂的　跌落的事物
在旁邊看一眼　只看一眼　渴望撫摸　肌膚相親
抱一次　只抱一次　渴望旋轉
現在只說遲到的愛，來得不是時候

（薛舟譯）

now only about love that came at the wrong time, too late

now about a thigh pierced by an awl rather than about
  the awl
about caked-dry eyelids and disfigured lips   about
  fresh mornings
in the congenial brothel, and the chill, less-heated side
  of the room
now about that one step that can't be taken so as to
  leave the congenial
brothel   about the slush road, the yawning
  chimney, and the sound of
a bell that flows along with the muddy water   about
  despoiled virgins
and the rotting arms and dried-out eyeballs of men
  who died untimely
now drunk on the fluid dreamy voices of older sisters
  and younger
sisters-in-law, drunk on the purple pattern of an
  abandoned seashell,
on the blue-green tail of a dead magpie on the road, I'll
  sing in tune

with the deep moans of all who go to their congenial
brothel, to homes
where there are parties, to homes mourning deaths of
all who blossom
and collapse   about wanting to see you once, just
once more, wanting
to touch you, to mesh our flesh, to be beside what's
been melted, bent,
frozen, split open, hurled aside   about wanting to
look at you once,
just once   and about wanting to hold you and to
whirl around holding you in my arms
now only about love that came at the wrong time, too
late

(Translated by Hye-jin Juhn Sidney & George Sidney)

7 序詩

간이식당에서 저녁을 사 먹었습니다
늦고 헐한 저녁이 옵니다
낯선 바람이 부는 거리는 미끄럽습니다
사랑하는 사람이여, 당신이 맞은편 골목에서
문득 나를 알아볼 때까지
나는 정처 없습니다

당신이 문득 나를 알아볼 때까지
나는 정처 없습니다
사방에서 새소리 번쩍이며 흘러내리고
어두워 가며 몸 뒤트는 풀밭,
당신을 부르는 내 목소리
키 큰 미류나무 사이로 잎잎이 춤춥니다

序詩

我在簡易餐廳吃晚飯
黃昏來臨，輕鬆而緩慢
陌生的風吹來，街道很滑
我愛的人啊，我無所適從
直到你在對面的巷子裏
突然認出我

我無所適從
直到你突然認出我
四周有鳥鳴閃爍和流淌
淩亂的草地越來越暗
我呼喚你的聲音
在高大的白楊樹間翩翩起舞

（薛舟譯）

prelude

I ate dinner at a snack bar
evening comes on, laggard and late
an unfamiliar wind slicks smooth the street
my love, until you of a sudden notice me
from where you are across the street
I won't know where I'm going

my love, until you of a sudden notice me
I won't know where I'm going
birds' sounds trill brightly all around
and the grass twists dark in the dusk
my voice, calling you,
dances among the rustling leaves of a tall poplar

(Translated by Hye-jin Juhn Sidney & George Sidney)

8 세월의 습곡이여, 기억의 단층이여

무엇과도 바꿀 수 없는 날들이 흘러갔다
강이 하늘로 흐를 때,
명절 떡쌀에 햇살이 부서질 때
우리가 아픈 것은 삶이 우리를
사랑하기 때문이다

무엇과도 바꿀 수 없는 날들이 흘러갔다
흐르는 안개가 아마포처럼 몸에 감길 때,
짐 실은 말 뒷다리가 사람 다리보다 아름다울 때
삶이 가엾다면 우린 거기
묶일 수밖에 없다

歲月的褶皺，記憶的斷層

任何事物都無法替換的日子流過
河水流向天空的時候
陽光碎在節日打糕米裏的時候
我們之所以痛苦　是因為生活
熱愛我們

任何事物都無法替換的日子流過
流淌的迷霧像亞麻布一樣纏住身體的時候
馱著貨物的馬的後退比人腿更美麗的時候
如果覺得生活可憐　那麼我們
只能被束縛在那裏

（薛舟譯）

the folding of time, the dislocation of memory

the days we wouldn't trade for anything have flowed by
when the river flows skyward,
when sunbeams are mashed into the rice for the
    holiday *ttok*,
the reason we're sick is that
life loves us

the days we wouldn't trade for anything have flowed by
when like linen the flowing fog enwraps our bodies,
when the hind legs of a horse, a load on its back, seem
    more
beautiful than human legs
even if we feel sorry for life we have no choice
but to be tied to it

(Translated by Hye-jin Juhn Sidney & George Sidney)

9 높이 치솟은 소나무 숲이

높이 치솟은 소나무숲이 불안하였다 밤, 하늘의 구
　름은 층층이 띠를 이루고 그 사이 하늘은 무
　늬 넓은 떡처럼 쌓였다 층층이, 하늘에 가
　면 말이 필요할까 이곳은 말이 통하지 않
　는 곳
이곳은 말이 통하지 않아! 집에 가면 오늘도 아버
　지 집에 낯선 사람들이 찾아온다 그들은 모
　두 피를 본 사람들이다 의로운 자들, 스스
　로 의롭게 여기는 자들의 입에 피가 묻어 있
　다 의로운 자들의 입에서 피가 웃는다 아버지
　는 그들을 몹시 사랑하신다
아, 하고 내 입에서 낮은 한숨이 나온다 오
　늘 밤 그들은 시끄러운 예언자를 묶어 나무
　에 매달 것이다 예언자도 그리 믿을 만한 사
　람은 못 된다 그의 배는 부르고 걱정이 없
　다 아무도 걱정하는 사람은 없고 ......
소나무 숲은 더욱 불안해진다 달이 소나무 숲으
　로 밀려가고 물은 움직이지 않는다

高聳的松林

高聳的松林躁動不安　夜晚，天上的雲層層相連
　　天空像花紋糕點堆積其間　一層層，天空需要
　　語言嗎　這裏語言不通
這裏語言不通！回家　今天又有陌生人來找父親
　　他們都是見過血的人　正義者，自以為正義的
　　人們嘴角有血　血在正義者的嘴裏微笑　父親
　　熱愛他們
啊，我低聲歎息　今天夜裏　他們捆綁多嘴的預言
　　家　吊上樹枝　預言家也不值得相信　他衣食
　　無憂　無所牽掛……
松林更加不安　月亮滑向松林　水靜止不動

（薛舟譯）

the forest of tall pine trees

the forest of tall pine trees was foreboding   night,
the clouds stacked up layer upon layer, strips of sky
in between like a layered rice cake   will words
be necessary in heaven   here words are not
understood
words are not understood here! today at home strangers
again come to visit our father   all of them have
spilled blood there is blood on the lips of these
righteous people, of these people who see themselves
as righteous   blood grins on the lips of these
righteous people   my father loves them very much
aah, a soft sigh escapes my mouth   tonight they
are going to tie up the prating prophet and hang
him from a tree   you can't even depend upon
a prophet   his stomach's full   he has no
worries   nobody's worried ...
the forest of pine trees looks even more foreboding
the moon's been blown toward the forest, and the
water is still

(Translated by Hye-jin Juhn Sidney & George Sidney)

10 신기하다, 신기해, 햇빛 찬연한 밤마다

어째서 산은 삼각형인가 어째서 물은 삼각형
　　으로 흐르지 않는가 어째서 여자 젖가슴
　　은 두 개뿐이고 어미 개의 젖가슴은 여덟 개
　　인가 언제부터 젖가슴은 무덤을 닮았는가 어
　　떻게 한 나무의 꽃들은 같은 색, 같은 무늬
　　를 가졌는가 어째서 달팽이는 딱딱한 껍질 속
　　에서 소리지르지 않고 귤껍질은 주황색으로 빛
　　나며 풀이 죽는가 귤껍질의 슬픔은 어디서 오
　　는가
어째서 병신들은 바로 걷지 못하고 전봇대는 완강
　　히 버티고 서 있는가 왜 해가 떠도 밤인가 매
　　일 밤 물오리는 어디에서 자는가 무슨 수
　　를 써서 조개는 멋진 껍질을 만드는가 왜 청
　　년들은 月經을 하지 않는가 어째서 동네 깡
　　패들은 의리에 죽고 의리에 사는가 왜 장님
　　은 앞을 못 보고 소방서에서는 불이 나지 않
　　는가 불에 타 죽어가는 새들은 무슨 말을 하
　　는가
왜 술 먹은 사람은 헛소리를 하고 술 안 먹은 사
　　람도 헛소리를 하는가 매일 밤 돌사자는 무
　　엇을 기다리는가 언제부터 風向計는 우두커

니 땅만 내려다보는가 어째서 귀여운 아이들
의 볼그레한 빰은 썩었는가 누가 소녀들의 가
랑이를 벌리고 말뚝을 박았는가 언제부터 창녀
들은 같은 길 같은 골목에서 서성거리고 초라
한 사내들은 어떻게 알고 찾아오는가
신기하다, 신기해, 햇빛 찬연한 밤마다 惡夢을 보
내주신 그대,
목마름을 다오! 身熱을 다오!

新奇啊，新奇，每個陽光燦爛的夜晚

山怎麼會是三角形　水為什麼不以三角形流淌　女人的乳房為什麼只有兩個　母狗的乳房卻有八個　從什麼時候開始乳房酷似墳墓　一棵樹的花為什麼同色同紋　蝸牛為什麼躲在硬殼裏不吭聲　桔子皮萎縮了為什麼是桔黃色　桔子皮的悲傷從何而來

瘸子為什麼不能正常走路　電線桿為什麼頑強挺立　為什麼太陽當空卻是夜晚　每天夜裏鴨子在哪兒睡覺　蛤蜊用什麼手段造出漂亮的外殼　為什麼小夥子不來月經　村裏的混混們為什麼生於義氣又死於義氣　盲人為什麼看不見前方　消防署為什麼不著火　被火燒死的鳥們說什麼

為什麼喝酒的人胡說八道　不喝酒的人也胡說八道　每天晚上石獅子在等什麼　從什麼時候開始風向標只是呆呆地俯視地面　可愛的孩子們紅通通的臉蛋為什麼腐爛　誰劈開少女的雙腿往裏打樁　從什麼時候開始妓女在同一條路同一條胡同裏徘徊　寒酸的男人們怎麼會沿路而來

新奇啊，新奇，每個陽光燦爛的夜晚送來惡夢的你，
賜我以渴！賜我以熱！

（薛舟譯）

amazing, how amazing it is, every night of the shining sun

why is the shape of a mountain triangular   why
  doesn't water flow in the shape of a triangle   why
  do women have only one pair of nipples, and bitches
  four   since when have breasts been shaped like
  burial mounds   how is it that a tree's blossoms are
  all of the same color and pattern   why don't snails
  rage out against their hard shells, and why does a
  tangerine's skin glow golden as it withers   what's
  the source of its sorrow
why can't the lame walk normally and why are electric
  power poles so obstinately erect   why is it night
  even after the sun rises   where do ducks sleep
  at night   by what means do mollusks create
  such ingenious shells   why don't young men
  menstruate   why do neighborhood thugs live
  for friendship and die for friendship   why can't
  the blind see and why isn't there fire in fire stations
  what do birds burning to death say
why do people who drink alcohol and also those who
  don't drink alcohol babble nonsense   what do

statuary stone lions wait for every night   since
when do wind vanes do nothing but stare down
at the ground   why do the pink cheeks of cute
children decay   who spread and rammed a rod
up between the legs of young girls   since when
have whores been hanging out on the same corners
of the same streets and how do their shabby johns
know where to look for them
amazing, how amazing it is   come, you who sent
me nightmares every night of the shining sun,
give me more thirst! Give my body more fever!

(Translated by Hye-jin Juhn Sidney & George Sidney)

11 수박

여름날 오후 뜨거운 언덕받이를 타고 아파트
로 가는 길엔 어른이나 아이나 제 머리통보
다 큰 수박 하나씩 비닐끈에 묶어 들고 땀 흘
리며, 땀 닦으며 정신없이 기어 오른다 그
들이 오르막 길에서 허우적거릴 땐 손에 달
린 수박이 떼구르르 구를 것도 같고, 굴러 내
려 쇠뭉치로 만든 공처럼 땅 속 깊이 묻혀 버
릴 것도 같지만 무사히, 무사히 수박은 개구
멍 같은 아파트 현관 속으로 들어간다
그럼 이제 어떤 일이 벌어지는가 우선 끈에 묶
인 수박을 풀고 간단히 씻은 다음, 검은 등
에 흰 배의 고등어 같은 부엌칼로 띵띵 부
은 수박의 배를 가르면, 끈적거리는 단물을 흘
리며 벌겋게 익은 속이 쩍, 갈라 떨어지고 쥐
똥 같은 검은 알이 튀어 나온다 그러면 저
마다 스텐 숟가락을 손에 쥔 아버지와 할머
니, 큰아이와 작은놈, 머리를 뒤로 묶은 딸아
이가 달겨들어 파먹기 시작하고, 언제나 뒷처
리하는 어머니는 이따금 숟가락 집어 거들기
도 하지만, 어머니는 입맛이 없다

어느새 수박씨는 마루 여기저기 흩어지고 허연 뱃대기를 드러낸 수박 껍데기가 깨진 사기 접시처럼 쌓일 때, 아이들은 자리를 박차고 뛰쳐 나가고 할머니는 건넌방에 드러눕고 아버지는 값싼 담배를 붙여 물고, 게으르고 긴 연기를 뿜을 것이다

그것은 어느 여름 어른들이 겪었다던 물난리 같은 것일까 질퍽하고 구질구질한 난장판 같은 것일까 아버지의 작업복을 기워 만든 걸레로 마루바닥을 훔치며 어머니는 바닥 여기저기 묻어 있는 수박물을 볼 것이다 벌건, 그러나 약간은 어둡고 끈끈한 수박물을...... 왠지 쓸쓸해지기만 하는 어떤 삶을......

西瓜

夏日午後　沿著炙熱的坡頂去公寓的路上　大人和
　　孩子都用塑膠繩提著比自己腦袋還大的西瓜
　　流汗　擦汗　努力往上爬　他們在上坡路苦苦
　　掙扎　提在手裏的西瓜好像要滾落　像鐵球深
　　埋在地裏　結果安然無恙　西瓜安然無恙　安
　　然無恙地進入狗洞般的公寓門
那麼　現在會有什麼事嗎　首先放下繩子捆住的西
　　瓜　簡單清洗　再用黑背白腹的鮐魚似的菜刀
　　切開圓滾滾的西瓜　流著黏稠的甜水　流出熟
　　透的紅瓤　濺出老鼠屎樣的黑籽　手握不鏽鋼
　　勺子的父親　祖母　大兒子和小兒子　頭髮紮
　　在後面的女兒跑來　狼吞虎嚥　總做善後的母
　　親偶爾拿起勺子　但是母親沒有胃口
轉眼間　地板上到處都是西瓜籽　露著白肚皮的西
　　瓜皮像破碎的瓷盤堆積起來　孩子們起身跑出
　　了門　祖母到隔壁躺下　父親點燃廉價香煙叼
　　在嘴裏　準備吐出慵懶而悠長的煙霧
像某年夏天大人們經歷的水災？還是泥濘而污穢的
　　混亂？母親用父親的工作服改成的抹布擦地板

看見滿地的西瓜汁　紅色的稍微黑暗和黏稠的
西瓜汁……怎麼有點兒像是淒涼的人生……

(薛舟譯)

watermelon

one summer afternoon on the hillside path up to the
apartment block families, children as well as
adults toil upward, sweating, wiping away the sweat,
each lugging a plastic twine-netted watermelon
larger than their heads as they grab at the air
for balance it seems that the melons dangling from
their hands will go rolling down the hill and like
balls of iron bury themselves at the bottom but
the melons make their way safely, safely into the
cubbyhole entrance of the building
now what happens the members of a family
first undo the twine they wash the melon
and with a kitchen knife resembling a black-
backed, white-bellied mackerel they split open the
swollen-to-bursting stomach sweet sticky juice
seeps from the ripe red insides, and black seeds
like rat droppings pop out then the father, the
grandmother, the first son, the second son, the pony-
tailed daughter, each wielding a stainless steel spoon
fall upon the melon and dig into it the mother,
who always finishes off whatever scraps remain, from

time to time lifts her spoon and joins them, but
without much appetite
finally, seeds strewn all about and pieces of naked
white belly-rind stacked up like porcelain dishes, the
children dash outside the grandmother lies down in
her room   the father lights a cheap cigarette and
blows out long lazy streams of smoke
is this similar to that calamitous flood the older people
tell us they lived through one summer   is it
similar to that turbid squalid mess wiping the floor
with a rag she'd made from the father's old work
clothes the mother comes upon watermelon juice
that's dribbled down here and there upon the floor,
watermelon juice, red, dark red, sticky ... a life of
deepening loneliness ...

(Translated by Hye-jin Juhn Sidney & George Sidney)

12 남해 금산

한 여자 돌 속에 묻혀 있었네
그 여자 사랑에 나도 돌 속에 들어갔네
어느 여름 비 많이 오고
그 여자 울면서 돌 속에서 떠나갔네
떠나가는 그 여자 해와 달이 끌어주었네
남해 금산 푸른 하늘가에 나 혼자 있네
남해 금산 푸른 바닷물 속에 나 혼자 잠기네

南海錦山

一個女人被埋進了石頭。
因為愛她我也走進了石頭
有一年夏天雨水很多
那個女人哭著從石頭裏離開
太陽和月亮指引著離去的女人
我獨自守著南海錦山蔚藍的天邊
我獨自潛入南海錦山蔚藍的海水

（薛舟譯）

South Sea, Silk Mountain

a woman was immured in stone
for her love I followed her into the stone
one summer it rained a lot
weeping, she left the stone
led by sun and moon she left
I'm alone now at the edge of the blue sky above Silk
   Mountain by the South Sea
alone I sink into the blue water of the South Sea at Silk
   Mountain

(Translated by Hye-jin Juhn Sidney & George Sidney)

李晟馥生於1952年，詩作極富想像力，層次豐富，一向備受注目，榮獲「金洙暎文學獎」及「素月詩歌文學獎」。李晟馥深受卡夫卡、尼采及波德萊爾影響，首部詩集《滾石何時醒來》中詩人充當臨床病理學家，剖析家庭和社會結構，並仔細記錄其逐漸瓦解的過程，聯想奔放大膽，戳破世界的虛偽、腐敗及墮落，深深震撼讀者。李晟馥的第二本詩集《南海錦山》源於他新近對東亞古典文學的興趣，大幅探討愛的本質。他在往後的詩集一直鑽研這個主題，為「愛」另造新語法，反映現代的情愛概念。詩人同時不斷求新，倡導詩歌改革，影響不少同期和年輕一代的詩人。

評論家金玹指李晟馥的詩作「大大擴展意義的領域，啟迪無盡的問題，問題不單局限於個人或私人層面，甚至擴闊至集體及公眾的層面。」李晟馥的詩作不斷遊走於兩個層面，展現人生底蘊中的基本關係。

李晟馥於首爾大學取得法國文學學士及碩士學位，曾任啟明大學法國文學系及創意寫作系教授。主要著作包括《滾石何時醒來》(1980)、《南海錦山》(1986)、《那年夏末》(1990)、《虎狼加時樹的回憶》(1993)、《啊，沒有嘴巴的東西！》(2003)、《月兒前額的波浪紋》(2003)、《來，看看悲傷就是全部》(2013)。

(謝小婷譯)

Lee Seong-bok (1952–), recipient of Kim Soo-young Literature Prize and Kim So-wol Literature Prize, has continually attracted attention to his highly imaginative and multi-layered poetry. Influenced by Kafka, Nietzsche and Baudelaire, Lee's first volume of poetry *When Do the Rolling Stones Awake* shocked readers with its daring use of free association to expose the hypocrisy, corruption and perversity of this world. In this volume, the poet occupies the place of a clinical pathologist who dissects familial and social structures, and meticulously records their gradual disintegration. His second book *Mt. Geum*, *Nahmae*, shaped by the poet's new interest in the East Asian classical literature, largely deals with the question of love's essence. The subject continues to engross Lee in subsequent volumes as well, and he creates an alternative grammar of love to the modern notion of romance. Driven by a spirit of innovation, Lee heralds a poetic revolution that influences both his contemporaries and younger generation of poets.

The critic Kim Hyoun has said of Lee Seong-bok's poetry that "it vastly expands its sphere of meaning to permit endless questions to be raised, not only on an individual or private level, but on the collective and public one as well." Moving unceasingly between binary categories, Lee's poetry thus brings into view the fundamental relation that lies beneath human life.

Lee earned both his undergraduate and graduate degrees in French literature from the Seoul National University. He worked as Professor of French literature and creative writing at the Keimyung University.

His major works include *When Do the Rolling Stones Awake* (Dwingguneun Dol-eun Eonje Jam Kkaeneunga, 1980), *South Sea, Silk Mountain* (Namhae Geumsan, 1986), *End of That Summer* (Geu Yeoreum-ui Kkeut, 1990), *Memories of the Holly* (Horanggasinamu-ui Gieok, 1993), *Oh, Those without Mouths* (A, Ib-I Eomneun Geotdeul, 2003), *Ripple Patterns on the Moon's Forehead* (Dal-ui Ima-eneun Mulgyeolmunui Jaguk, 2003), *Came, and Saw Sorrow Was All* (Rae Yeo Ae Ban Da Ra, 2013).

出版 Publisher
香港中文大學出版社 The Chinese University Press

封面影像 Cover Image
北島 Bei Dao

出版日期 Date of Publication
二零一三年十一月 November 2013

國際書號 ISBN
978-962-996-615-7

香港國際詩歌之夜 2013 International Poetry Nights in Hong Kong 2013
主辦單位 Organizers
香港中文大學文學院 Faculty of Arts, The Chinese University of Hong Kong
香港浸會大學文學院 Faculty of Arts, Hong Kong Baptist University
香港科技大學人文社會科學學院 School of Humanities and Social Science, The Hong Kong University of Science and Technology

合作夥伴 In Partnership With
英國文化協會 British Council

協辦單位 Co-organizers
時刻文化 Moment Communications
香港中文大學出版社 The Chinese University Press

贊助 Sponsors
香港兆基創意書院 HKICC Lee Shau Kee School of Creativity
中國會 The China Club
周凱旋基金會 Chau Hoi Shuen Foundation

Printed in Hong Kong